Willa Cather

Willa Cather

A PICTORIAL MEMOIR

Photographs by Lucia Woods *and others*

Text by Bernice Slote

UNIVERSITY OF NEBRASKA PRESS · LINCOLN

Publishers on the Plains
UNP

Copyright © 1973 by the University of Nebraska Press
All rights reserved
Library of Congress Catalog Card Number 72–91511
International Standard Book Number 0–8032–0828–6

Designed by Michael Stancik
Manufactured in the U.S.A. by R. R. Donnelley & Sons Company
Chicago, Illinois, and Crawfordsville, Indiana

To Mildred Rhoads Bennett

Author, Conservator, Researcher —
who, in four decades of study, service, and leadership,
has greatly enlarged our understanding
of Willa Cather's life and works

Contents

When Willa Cather was born in 1873, vast regions of America were still to be settled and shaped; ahead were bright possibilities. When she died in 1947, after a career as journalist, editor, and fiction writer, her country was lived in, but, scarred by two World Wars and periodic depressions, it was older than its age. In her novels and short stories she had captured the qualities of life and feeling that had glorified and disturbed Americans during the nearly fifty years she was creating fiction.

Willa Cather's imaginative world was one of subtle human relationships in settings of extraordinary physical reality—not only the land of Nebraska pioneers but also the Southwest, Quebec, the cities and islands of the East, and Virginia. Rarely have those regions, especially the Midlands and the Southwest, been given such pictorial life and brilliance as in her novels. The colors and shapes and voices of the land are there, not reported but recreated through her own sensibility and by the translating hand into the truth of art. She used regional materials not to show differences or to sketch local color but because they were her deepest emotional resources, and in them she embodied universal themes.

Willa Cather's union of life and art is suggested in the pages of this book. Some of her own vivid memories are combined in Part I with views of persons and places that made up the texture of her life. Part II—"Willa Cather's America"—focuses on the sense of place in her novels, with three pictorial essays entitled "The Midlands," "The Southwest," and "The Northeast and the South." These pictures are not intended to illustrate the books but to offer visual images of response and illumination that may then recombine for the reader in new ways. I have chosen to emphasize the American landscape because I agree with Dorothy Canfield

Fisher's definition of Willa Cather as "deeply and mystically our own." According to Mrs. Fisher, writing in the *New York Herald-Tribune* in 1933, Willa Cather was "the only American author who has concentrated on the only unique quality of our national life"— the effect a new country has on the lives of those who come to it. One might add that no one has captured so vividly such a variety of regions in America; the idea transcended limitations of place.

Neither symbolic nor representative, Willa Cather is one American artist who made her way through the diversity and bewilderment of American life to interpretations and some reconciliations. Whatever she found of chaos is balanced by something achieved, something understood. The key, as she wrote in *My Ántonia,* is to "become a part of something entire." Or, as in the lines on her tombstone: "That is happiness; to be dissolved into something complete and great."

BERNICE SLOTE

University of Nebraska–Lincoln

I. Willa Cather

Virginia

Willa Cather was born on December 7, 1873, in Back Creek Valley, near Gore, Virginia. Since Revolutionary times, Cathers had lived in the farming and sheep-raising hills and meadows of northern Virginia, near the long green valley of the Shenandoah. Her people on her mother's side were the Boaks and the Seiberts, some of whom came from what is now West Virginia; her grandfather William Boak served three times in the Virginia House of Delegates. On both sides it was a strong, religious, public-spirited, often political ancestry. Her parents, Mary Virginia Boak and Charles Fectigue Cather, were married in 1872, only seven years after the end of the Civil War. Still, even with a divisive war in close memory, the Virginia world Willa Cather knew until she was nine and a half years old was a secure one, with well-built, spacious houses looking out toward the Blue Ridge Mountains; with thick, leafy roads through the Hollow, the sound of spring water flowing, and rabbit traps that stayed where she placed them. From this world Willa Cather moved with her family when they went by rail in April 1883 to settle where her grandparents, the William Cathers, and her uncle George and his wife had gone some years before—in the wide, raw, new country of the western plains, in Webster County, Nebraska. What she wrote about most was her Nebraska growing-up, but her earliest—her Virginia—childhood was always alive at the source of Willa Cather's experience, the beginning of the memories she transmuted into art.

Willa Cather's birthplace, the home of her grandmother, Rachel Elisabeth Boak

Charles F. Cather

Mary Virginia Boak Cather

5

Willow Shade, on the road from Winchester to Romney

In the fall of 1874 the Charles Cathers and their baby daughter moved to Willow Shade, built by Charles's father, William Cather, before the Civil War. They lived here until they moved to Nebraska in the spring of 1883. The four-story barn, shown opposite, housed a mill for the sheep fattened at Willow Shade and marketed in Baltimore.

The sheepbarn at Willow Shade. Willa in loft door (see blow-up at right)

Willa, aged about nine

Back Creek Valley, Virginia

"I would not know," Willa Cather said in 1913, "how much a child's life is bound up in the woods and hills and meadows around it, if I had not been jerked away from all these and thrown out into a country as bare as a piece of sheet iron." As they rode by wagon north from Red Cloud through clawed-out places into the high, flat part of Webster County called the Divide—an unshaped, unhuman land—her father told her that one must show grit in a new country. When the larks sang their "few splendid notes" Willa thought she would "go under." But the strangeness faded into ploughed fields and young orchards, into the tall red grass and the great sky that reshaped her life.

Virgin prairie, Webster County, Nebraska

"It was over flat lands like this, stretching out to drink the sun,
that the larks sang—and one's heart sang there, too. . . .
There was a new song in that blue air which had never been sung
in the world before."

"Trees were so rare in that country, and they had to make such a hard fight
to grow, that we used to feel anxious about them, and visit them
as if they were persons. It must have been the scarcity of detail in that
tawny landscape that made detail so precious."

Site of the Cather homestead, the Divide, Webster County

On the rise at the left was the frame house built by the William Cathers in 1877. Other Virginians had settled nearby in Catherton Precinct, but around them were many immigrant families from Europe and French Canada.

In Willa Cather's first known composition, she argued the superiority of dogs over cats. Shown here is the first of the four pages of the essay.

Essay entitled "Dogs"

The Dane Church, Webster County

"The early population of Nebraska was largely transatlantic. . . .
On Sunday we could drive to a Norwegian church and listen to a sermon
in that language, or to a Danish or a Swedish church. We could go to the
French Catholic settlement in the next county and hear a sermon
in French, or into the Bohemian township and hear one in Czech, or we
could go to church with the German Lutherans. There were, of course,
American congregations also."

Red Cloud from the north

"Little towns like these, buried in wheat and corn . . . ."

By the spring of 1885 the Cather family had moved to Red Cloud, some sixteen miles south of the Divide. They settled in a modest, rambling, white frame house a block from Webster Street, where Charles Cather opened an office to deal with abstracts, loans, and mortgages—an office in which Willa learned to be helpful. Red Cloud was a promising town, a division point of the Burlington and Missouri railroad on the main line from Kansas City to Denver, and through it came the private cars of the railroad aristocracy. The bustle and clangor and drama of railroading pervaded the town, and always there were the yearning whistles of express trains in the night.

Near the Cathers lived the James Miner family (the Miners become the Harlings in *My Ántonia*), owners of the big general store a block away, and the clothier Charles Wiener and his wife, of a cultured European background (the Rosens in "Old Mrs. Harris"). The Cathers went to the Baptist Church, saw plays at the Opera House, were Republican through all political quarrels. By the end of the 1880's their family consisted of parents and five children, Grandma Boak, Cousin Bess Seymour, and Marjorie Anderson, a housemaid who had come with them from Virginia.

Though Carrie Miner was four years older, she became Willa's closest friend. Together the Miner and Cather children (and others) explored the fields around the town, adventured on the bluffs and sandbars of the Republican River a mile south, and crossed Crooked Creek to the east to wander in the Garber cottonwood grove, where the trees were planted evenly in rows and blended to a deep, cool shade. They built a play-town (Willa was mayor), marched in parades, and performed on improvised stages. At the

Willa Cather in her early teens

Opera House they presented *Beauty and the Beast* on February 6, 1888, in a benefit for victims of the great January 12 blizzard (see page 25).

In 1886, when James Cather was born, Mrs. Cather was too ill to tend Willa's curls, so Willa marched to the barber and had her hair cut like a boy's. From this time until her second year in university she dressed as much like a boy as she could: her wardrobe included a derby and a stetson as well as the Civil War cap shown in the tintype above. In her teens Willa helped her doctor friends (she sometimes signed herself "William Cather, M.D."), climbed windmills on visits to the Divide, collected seashells, performed scientific experiments, and read, and read.

Willa Cather was graduated from Red Cloud High School in 1890, in a class of three. Her Commencement oration was lyrical, and, for a girl of sixteen, profound. Called "Superstition vs. Investigation," it was about the human race in history and its search for truth.

The Cather home at Third and Cedar streets

". . . a low storey-and-a-half house, with a wing built on at the right and
a kitchen addition at the back, everything a little on the slant—roofs,
windows, and doors."

Red Cloud

Bird's-eye view of
RED CLOUD
Webster County, Nebraska, 1881

(1) Republican River, south of Red Cloud
(2) Burlington & Missouri railroad and depot
(3) Garber ("Forrester") residence and
    cottonwood grove (*A Lost Lady*)
(4) Crooked Creek (*The Song of the Lark, A Lost Lady*)
(5) Boys' Home Hotel (*My Ántonia*)
(6) Miner Store at Third and Webster
    ("Two Friends")
(7) Cather home at Third and Cedar (*The Song of
    the Lark,* "Old Mrs. Harris," "The Best Years")
(8) Miner ("Harling") home (*My Ántonia*)
(9) Courthouse (*The Song of the Lark, One of Ours*)
(10) Methodist Church (*The Song of the Lark*)

Drawn by Augustus Koch

Webster Street, looking south

Webster Street was the scene of an 1889 political rally for William
Jennings Bryan, who was elected to Congress the following year.
By the clock in the foreground is Dr. Henry Cook's drugstore,
where Willa often worked. The tall building is the Farmers and
Merchants Bank, built in 1889 by Governor Silas Garber (the
prototype for Captain Forrester in *A Lost Lady*).

Roscoe (Ross) Cather (b. 1877), by the Miner store

Douglass Cather (b. 1880)

Jessica Cather (b. 1881)

James Cather (b. 1886)

21

During Willa Cather's childhood in Red Cloud, her family attended the Baptist Church. Both the Baptist and the Methodist churches reappear in later fiction.

The Baptist Church, Red Cloud

The State Bank Building, Red Cloud

The State Bank, on the corner of Webster and Fourth streets, was built in 1885. In the same block, to the north, was the Opera House, also built in 1885. There Willa Cather delivered her Commencement oration.

To Willa Cather, the music of organ and voices at the Catholic Church was art — beautiful and rich with the sense of the past. She often attended mass with Carrie Miner, seen opposite in her riding habit. The picture is similar to one which stood on Willa Cather's desk all her life. Above is a picture of Willa (right), with Evelyn Brodstone, the future Lady Vestey, and Margie Miner.

St. Juliana Falconieri, Red Cloud

Willa and friends, 1890

Facade of the Red Cloud Opera House

Carrie Miner

Cast of Beauty and the Beast; *Willa in top hat*

25

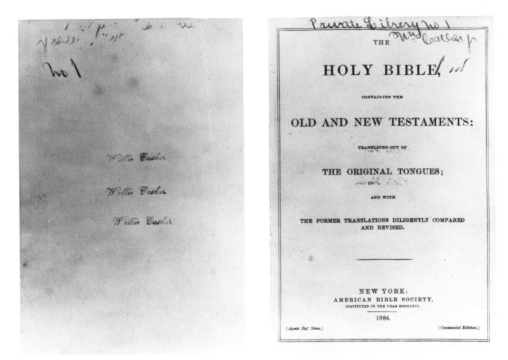

Willa Cather's Bible

As Willa Cather began to collect her own books, she labeled and numbered a series of them "Private Library" of "Wm Cather Jr." The title page of an 1884 King James Bible, shown above, is marked "No. 1." The facing page has some ink blots at the top, and "Willie Cather" stamped in blue three times in the center. Among other "Private Library" books are Upham's *Abridgement of Mental Philosophy* (No. 5), Bunyan's *Pilgrim's Progress* (No. 14), and Alcott's *Jo's Boys* (No. 21).

In the center of a continent, on plains once an inland sea still marked by traces of fish and shell, Willa Cather heard the murmur of seashells brought from far away. These are from her own collection.

Seashells in Willa's room

Willa's room in the house at Third and Cedar

Willa Cather's room in a wing of the attic had a low, sloping ceiling, a double window that went to the floor, and wallpaper she had put on herself—"small red and brown roses on a yellowish ground." A lantern stood on a hat-crate at the head of her bed. The room, with its original wallpaper, has been recreated in the Cather house in Red Cloud from descriptions in *The Song of the Lark* and "The Best Years."

The Republican River

The river with its islands and willows and shifting currents was a realm of imagination and dreams. In *April Twilights* the first poem refers to Willa and her brothers Ross and Douglass as "three who lay and planned at moonrise, / On an island in a western river, / Of the conquest of the world together."

The River Road

"There is another book of God than that of scriptural revelation," Willa Cather declared in her Commencement oration, "a book written in the chapters of creation upon the pages of the universe bound in mystery." Later, she would write of "the solemn magic that comes out of those fields at nightfall."

The University Years

Louise Pound and Willa Cather

Willa Cather attended the University of Nebraska for five years, including a preparatory year, and was graduated in 1895. When she arrived in 1890, Lincoln and the university were just over twenty years old. Lincoln was an island of transplanted culture surrounded by sunflowers, red grass, prairie fires, and newly broken land. From the high ground at the edge of town she could see the evening star suspended "in the utter clarity of the western slope." She studied mostly classics and literature, taught by men from Harvard, Johns Hopkins, Sweden's University of Gothenberg. Among her friends and associates were others destined for fame: philologist Louise Pound, jurist Roscoe Pound, novelist Dorothy Canfield Fisher (daughter of James Canfield, NU chancellor, 1891-1895). Other special friends were Mariel, Frances, and Ellen Gere, daughters of Charles H. Gere, publisher and editor of the *Nebraska State Journal.* Willa Cather joined clubs, acted in plays, boosted football, and edited campus publications, especially the *Hesperian.* In it are many of her early stories. After 1893 she worked professionally for the *Journal,* whose managing editor was Will Owen Jones. Like the new city, the new university, Willa Cather in those years was something of a prodigy—a young girl who could write better than anybody. She will make her mark, they said.

The University of Nebraska campus in 1892

The Hesperian *staff, 1892–93.
The editor, Paul Pizey, center,
next to Willa Cather,
then literary editor*

Nebraska State Journal *building; University campus in background*

From 1893 to 1897, and occasionally later, Willa Cather wrote play reviews, features, and a column on the arts for the *Journal*. Lincoln had two large theatres showing a hundred-odd plays a year, with stars like Mansfield, Marlowe, Modjeska, Joseph Jefferson; and Lincoln had Willa Cather, with an ever widening reputation as a brilliant, slashing drama critic.

Will Owen Jones

"Art is not thought or emotion, but
expression, expression, always expression.
To keep an idea living, intact, tinged with
all its original feeling, its original mood,
preserving in it all the ecstasy which attended
its birth, to keep it so all the way from the
brain to the hand and transfer it on paper
a living thing with color, odor, sound,
life all in it, that is what art means, that is the
greatest of all the gifts of the gods.
And that is the voyage perilous."

Willa at her desk at the Journal

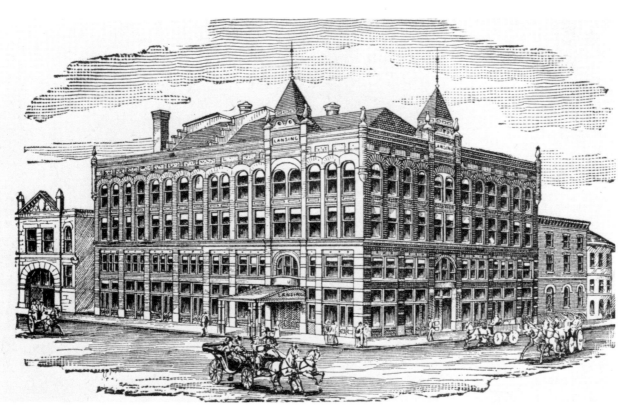

The Lansing Theatre, Lincoln

In 1894 Willa Cather posed as Electra in a tableau, part of a program of Latin and Greek plays. Closing other distances, in March 1895 she went to Chicago for a week of grand opera. The intensity of the experience is reflected in later novels. It is at an Auditorium concert that Thea Kronborg (*The Song of the Lark*) first hears Dvořák's "New World Symphony"; in the Arts Building is Clement Sebastian's studio (*Lucy Gayheart*). Chicago Historical Society photograph.

In June 1895

Willa as Electra, 1894

Michigan Avenue, 1900: The Auditorium, the Studebaker Building (later known as the Fine Arts Building), and the Chicago Club

Picnic in Red Cloud, 1895. Back row: Irene Miner, Elsie, Willa, and Roscoe Cather.
Front row: Frances and Ellen Gere, Jessica Cather, Margie Miner, Douglass Cather

Elsie Cather (b. 1890)

John (Jack) Cather (b. 1892)

ENTERED IN THE POST OFFICE AT LINCOLN
AS SECOND-CLASS MATTER.

PUBLISHED EVERY SATURDAY

-- —BY— --

THE COURIER PRINTING AND PUBLISHING CO.

Office 217 North Eleventh St.

Telephone 384

W. MORTON SMITH	Editor and Manager
SARAH B. HARRIS	Associate Editor
WILLA CATHER	Associate Editor

Sarah B. Harris

W. Morton Smith

From 1895 to 1900 Willa Cather contributed to the *Courier,* a Lincoln weekly. She was an associate editor during the summer and fall of 1895, working with her friends Sarah B. Harris (later editor of the paper) and W. Morton Smith, a fine young newspaperman, and as near to a rival as she had in Lincoln. In 1897 he was drowned in a boating accident on the Hudson River.

Union Station

Willa Cather came to Pittsburgh in June 1896 to edit a small magazine, the *Home Monthly.* For the next twenty years she would be coming and going through the Pittsburgh railroad station. On a hill nearby loomed Central High School, where she would teach for a time.

The Home Monthly *office (left) in the East Liberty section of Pittsburgh*

Willa Cather edited the *Home Monthly* during 1896-97, contributed to other company publications, and reviewed plays for the *Pittsburgh Leader.* From 1897 to 1900 she worked full time as telegraph editor, drama critic, and book reviewer on the *Leader;* later she also wrote for the *Library* and the *Gazette.* At first she lived in a series of boardinghouses; one of them is seen opposite. After a winter freelancing in Washington, D.C. (1900-1901), she taught for over five years in the Pittsburgh and Allegheny high schools. Willa Cather had many friends in the city's newspaper, library, theatrical, and musical worlds, but she came to be closest to Isabelle McClung, whom she met in 1898-99. She also admired the Pittsburgh composer Ethelbert Nevin, whose early death in 1901 affected her deeply. But Pittsburgh, even with its soot and darkness at noon and its flaring steel furnaces by night, was filled with energy and artistic aspiration, and it became the crucible of Willa Cather's first books—the poems of *April Twilights* (1903) and the stories of *The Troll Garden* (1905).

Isabelle McClung

Ethelbert Nevin in his studio

Willa Cather lived in this boardinghouse at 304 South Craig, not far from the Carnegie Library

The McClung house, 1180 Murray Hill Avenue, Pittsburgh

At Isabelle's invitation, Willa Cather lived with the family of Judge Samuel A. McClung from 1901 to the spring of 1906, when she took a position on *McClure's Magazine* in New York. Until the household was dissolved when Isabelle married Jan Hambourg in 1916, Willa returned for long visits. In the foreground of this picture is Ellen McClung Stone, Isabelle's grandniece.

St. Ouen, Rouen

In 1902 Willa and Isabelle spent the summer abroad. The factual account is in published letters; creatively, the journey into the Old World emerges in later fiction. Musing on the distance that light travels from its source, Claude Wheeler (*One of Ours*) thinks that "the purple and crimson and peacock-green" of St. Ouen's rose window had been shining for centuries before it reached him. "He felt distinctly that it went through him and farther still."

A favorite spot for Willa Cather was Avignon and its Palace of the Popes. "Her most splendid memory," wrote her friend Elizabeth Shepley Sergeant, "was of the Rocher des Doms and its Virgin, golden above the great river." Her last, unfinished, story was set in Avignon. In Paris she frequented the Luxembourg Gardens and the nearby Pantheon with its frescoes of the life of St. Geneviève.

Palace of the Popes, Avignon

Luxembourg Gardens with view of the Pantheon, Paris

Douglass Cather as a station agent, Cheyenne

Willa and Ross in Cheyenne

The Burlington & Missouri depot, Red Cloud

"How smoothly the trains run beyond the Missouri;/Even in my sleep I know when I have crossed the river." Nearly every year Willa Cather returned to Red Cloud and the familiar depot, often traveling west as far as Cheyenne, where Douglass worked as a station agent. Some small towns and lonely farms (overleaf) reappear in "The Sculptor's Funeral" and "A Wagner Matinee" in *The Troll Garden*— a book which led her to New York at last.

Barnyard, Webster County

Dinner in honor of Mark Twain's birthday, The Delmonico, New York, December 5, 1905.
Left to right: Frederick A. Duneka, Willa Cather, Edward S. Martin

Washington Square at the turn of the century

In late April 1903 Willa Cather was invited to New York by the dynamic and innovative publisher S. S. McClure, who then arranged to publish *The Troll Garden;* thus began a relationship of many years. Not until the spring of 1906, however, when key staff members left *McClure's,* did she go to New York to work on the magazine. In those early days she lived first at 60 Washington Square, then, along with Edith Lewis, a friend from Lincoln, at 82 Washington Place; these rooming houses are described in "Coming, Aphrodite!" By 1906 cities were not new to her any more. Perhaps that is why she places the New York of some short stories and *My Mortal Enemy* several years earlier, when its feel was younger, more magnetic, more mysterious. But in the orderly gardens, the glittering streets, and the hum of the crowds New York was the world, indeed, and what she had waited for.

Willa Cather on the staff of McClure's   *S. S. McClure around* 1900

Willa Cather's first major assignment at *McClure's* was to edit a biography of Mary Baker Eddy, so she spent much of 1907 in Boston, becoming a close friend of Mrs. James T. Fields, famed for her literary salon, and the writer Sarah Orne Jewett. In 1908 she traveled in Italy with Isabelle McClung, was made managing editor of *McClure's*. Willa Cather and McClure made a good team: both had been immigrants to the West, both had fiery imaginations, though she added a kind of order and efficiency he lacked. Several times after 1908 she went abroad on manuscript business; *McClure's* published the best English and American writers. Its offices were near Madison Square, the part of New York Willa Cather used for central scenes in *My Mortal Enemy*, along with some figures who breathed a still different air: Diana stepping high above Madison Square; the great Polish actress Modjeska sitting like Queen Katherine in the Henshawe living room.

"Madison Square . . . seemed to me so neat, after the raggedness of our Western cities; so protected by good manners and courtesy—like an open-air drawing-room."

Madison Square and the second Madison Square Garden

Mme Helena Modjeska

"She sat by the fire in a high-backed chair, her head resting lightly on her hand, her beautiful face half in shadow. How well I remember those long, beautifully modelled hands, . . . hands to hold a sceptre, or a chalice—or, by courtesy, a sword."

Going by train into Red Cloud Willa Cather would see the river bluffs of her childhood. Remembering the place, and the imagined mesas of the Southwest, she wrote "The Enchanted Bluff"(1909) and moved toward the future. In Boston, at the Fields house on Charles Street, she absorbed the elegance, the lively authority, of a tradition that would never be wholly the past.

Chalk cliff south of Red Cloud

"'There's the white chalk cliff where the Indians used to run the buffalo over Bison Leap—we kids called it—the remote sea wall of the boy world.'"

The library at 148 Charles Street. At left, in the window, Mrs. James T. Fields; at right, by the fireplace, Sarah Orne Jewett

"At 148 Charles Street an American of the Apache period and territory could come to inherit a Colonial past."

During 1912 *McClure's* published as a serial *Alexander's Masquerade* (later titled *Alexander's Bridge*) and "The Bohemian Girl," a long story admired for its new subject matter, the immigrants of Nebraska farming country, drawn with great vitality in Breughel-like portraits. It is a common error to think of this story and the 1913 novel *O Pioneers!* as Willa Cather's first use of what she later called her own subject matter. Nearly half of her short stories between 1892 and 1912 are set in Nebraska. Some are stark individual dramas of adjustment in the new West ("Peter," "On the Divide"); others, anticipating Sinclair Lewis by fifteen years, are critical of middle-class, small-town values. ("The Sculptor's Funeral," however, is more than matched by the attack on materialism in the 1911 New York story, "Behind the Singer Tower.") She often showed the West stronger than the East, as in the passionate "Eric Hermannson's Soul," and wrote affectionate memoirs in "Tommy, the Unsentimental" and "The Enchanted Bluff." Both these stories and others of Eastern cities ("Paul's Case") often have similar themes of the growth, or destruction, of personalities. *Alexander's Bridge*, a study of a man torn between his present and his past, is psychologically also Cather's "own material," though it is set in Boston, London, Paris; the worlds of society and the theatre. Alexander's maturity is with American bridges, and with his wife in the long drawing rooms near Charles Street in Boston. His young life, symbolized by actress Hilda Burgoyne, returns with London stages and the houses of Bloomsbury, near the British Museum. The division of two times, two places, mirrors Willa Cather's own pulls of East and West, the complexities of desire.

Charles Street, Boston

In Boston, Charles Street is reflected in the window of an antique shop.

In London, a garden is enclosed in Bloomsbury, near the British Museum and its "vaulted cold" which made "one's hour of youth the more precious."

Bloomsbury, London

Willa Cather as managing editor of McClure's

"The best magazine executive I know is Miss Cather," S. S. McClure once said. But Sarah Orne Jewett, before her death in 1909, had urged her friend to find her "own quiet centre of life," to "deepen and enrich" her work. After a leave of absence in 1911 and later a trip to Arizona, by the end of 1912 there was *Alexander's Bridge,* with *O Pioneers!* soon to come. Willa Cather had changed from editor to novelist.

Douglass Cather and a friend, Walnut Canyon, Arizona

Willa Cather's first four novels were published by Houghton Mifflin: *Alexander's Bridge* (1912), *O Pioneers!* (1913), *The Song of the Lark* (1915), and *My Ántonia* (1918). She felt good about *O Pioneers!*, believing that in this free, easy-moving Whitmanesque book of the varied strands of pioneer America she had at last "hit the home pasture." Some of her new creative freedom came from her encounter with the Southwest, where she visited her brother Douglass in 1912. In a sense Arizona repeated her childhood Nebraska—a wide, lonely, unfinished landscape—but this was a world sensibly more primitive, more anciently civilized. Once she had merely felt the "yearning of all flat lands"; now she was stirred by the drama of desert horizons. Arizona's Walnut Canyon, with its remains of cliff dwellers, becomes Panther Canyon in an important section of *The Song of the Lark*, a story of Willa Cather's own childhood blended with the career of a Wagnerian opera star like her friend Olive Fremstad.

Cornfield on the Divide, Webster County, Nebraska

In these years Willa Cather made numerous trips to the West, where seasons and weather plainly revolved in cycles of life and death. Sometimes, when horizons circled too far, she had to escape from bigness—"for fear of dying in a cornfield," reports Elizabeth Sergeant. *Why?* "You could not understand. You have not seen those miles of fields. There is no place to hide in Nebraska. You can't hide under a windmill."

Virgin prairie south of Red Cloud

But she also found rock mesas rising with shadow in the desert, and in Nebraska the flickering cottonwoods, green and golden. The roots of the tall, branching cottonwood (the pioneers' tree, she said) drank deep from hidden waters, deep in the soil where bones of dinosaurs lay. The waters of ancient springs had been found on the virgin prairie, springs so old that Coronado, coming north this far, might have drunk from them.

Elizabeth Shepley Sargeant in 1913

Mrs. Jan Hambourg (Isabelle McClung)

Willa Cather's friendship with the writer Elizabeth Sergeant, shown in Arlésienne dress, began in 1910. *The Song of the Lark,* dedicated to Isabelle McClung, derived in part from the career of Olive Fremstad, a friend since 1913.

Olive Fremstad as Sieglinde in Die Walküre

Willa Cather at Mesa Verde, 1915

Willa Cather explored Mesa Verde for the first time in 1915, dressed in khaki and glowing like a girl of the Golden West. In the houses and artifacts of the cliff dwellers, ordered and beautiful even in their ruin, she found a permanent symbol of man's long striving for life and art. She and Edith Lewis once were lost, and rescued, after a night in the Mesa Verde canyons. All these experiences began to fuse into what, ten years later, would be "Tom Outland's Story" in *The Professor's House.*

Mount Monadnock from the Old Cemetery, Jaffrey Center, New Hampshire, as it appeared in 1947

In the New York apartment at 5 Bank Street which she shared with Edith Lewis from 1913 to 1927, Willa Cather worked well. From 1915 to 1920 she published eight short stories of artists and city life; like the four novels of the period, this fiction embodied various forms and techniques. Another favorite spot was Jaffrey, New Hampshire. She first vacationed there in 1917 with Jan and Isabelle Hambourg and often returned to the Shattuck Inn for a month or two. When Willa Cather was buried in Jaffrey's old graveyard in 1947, Edith Lewis took a picture of Mount Monadnock as it could then be seen rising in blue haze beyond the woods —a little like North Mountain in Willa's early Virginia.

Part of *My Ántonia* was written in a tent set up in a meadow near the Shattuck Inn, on a farm called High Mowing. Each morning Willa Cather walked through the woods to the tent.

Her small room in the Shattuck Inn was on the top floor, just under the roof. It had sloping walls and a window looking out over the New Hampshire woods and meadows.

*Lt. G. P. Cather,
prototype of
Claude Wheeler*

World War I troopship passing the Statue of Liberty

"The scene was ageless; youths were sailing away to die for an idea,
a sentiment, for the mere sound of a phrase . . . and on their departure
they were making vows to a bronze image in the sea."

Although it is now considered the classic Cather novel—perhaps
her best—*My Ántonia* received less initial attention than some
of her other books because it appeared in the hectic days of World
War I. Yet at that time H. L. Mencken called her one of the best
of all American novelists. Achievement was balanced by loss—her
cousin Lt. G. P. Cather killed in action. This war seemed to her
the last in a long movement of men and blood back through the
Civil War and far beyond to the black ships of the Greeks and
Trojans.

Willa Cather in 1920

"Art, it seems to me, should simplify. That, indeed, is very nearly the whole of the higher artistic process; finding what conventions of form and what detail one can do without and yet preserve the spirit of the whole—so that all that one has suppressed and cut away is there to the reader's consciousness as much as if it were in type on the page."

By 1920 Willa Cather had turned to a new publisher, Alfred A. Knopf, a young man of taste and energy, who became a lifelong friend. Knopf issued the last thirteen of her books in beautiful formats: the first volume, a collection of short stories, *Youth and the Bright Medusa* (1920), was followed by *One of Ours* in 1922. The story of Claude Wheeler received mixed reviews, but in 1923 it was awarded the Pulitzer Prize. Willa Cather heard the news at Ville d'Avray, near Paris, where she was visiting the Hambourgs. She had also spent some time in France in 1920, researching the work. In both Claude's story and her own experience she had made a bridge between the Old and New Worlds, linking America with France.

Willa Cather at Cavalière, Provence

*Grave of Lt. G. P. Cather,
killed in action at Cantigny, May 28, 1918*

Willa Cather and Isabelle Hambourg at Ville d'Avray, 1923

Willa Cather in the Luxembourg Gardens

The next decade meant rich achievement. During the high tide of her work in the 1920s, some thought Cather's Nebraska novel of fading dreams—*A Lost Lady* (1923)—was her best; others chose *Death Comes for the Archbishop* (1927), a brilliant tapestry woven of legend and history in the Southwest. Between them came *The Professor's House* (1925) and *My Mortal Enemy* (1926), psychological dramas of the self as it faces mortality. *Shadows on the Rock* (1931), about early Quebec, affirmed man's pioneer efforts to preserve life, physical and spiritual. In 1923 *April Twilights* was reissued with new poems added, and there followed several distinguished short stories using memories of Pittsburgh and Nebraska: "Uncle Valentine" (1925), "Double Birthday" (1929), and "Neighbour Rosicky" (1930).

For Elsie, a picture of Bakst
and me in his beautiful studio.

Paris, October 1, 1923   Willa Cather

In 1923 the Omaha Society of Fine Arts com-
missioned a portrait of Willa Cather, to hang
in the Omaha Public Library. For the artist
she chose Leon Bakst, noted scene designer for
the Russian Ballet, and sat for him in Paris.

The Bakst portrait

Dorothy Canfield Fisher

Zoë Akins

Friends of McClure's Magazine *days: S. S. McClure, Willa Cather, Ida M. Tarbell, and Will Irwin, 1924*

During the twenties Willa Cather held and renewed many old friendships—with the novelist Dorothy Canfield Fisher for one. Close to her also was Zoë Akins, the witty and successful playwright, whom she had known and encouraged for a decade earlier. With Edith Lewis she began vacationing on Grand Manan, New Brunswick, and in the mid-twenties they built a cottage of their own on that rocky island in the Bay of Fundy.

Cather Cottage, Grand Manan, N. B., snapped by the carpenter

"Restlessness such as ours, success such as ours, striving such as ours, do not make for beauty. Other things must come first, good cookery, cottages that are homes, not playthings; gardens, repose."

A Santa Fe garden often visited by Willa Cather

Willa Cather at Grand Manan

On a hike

"She walks with the gait of one who
has been used to the saddle.
Her complexion is firm with an
outdoor wholesomeness. The red
in her cheeks is the red that comes
from the bite of the wind.
Her voice is deep, rich, and full of
color; she speaks with her whole
body, like a singer."

In conversation

Another snapshot by Edith Lewis

67

Portrait by Steichen

Below, an oil painting of Willa Cather done in Santa Fe by Nikolai Fechin. It hung in her Park Avenue apartment.

One of the most familiar Cather portraits is a smiling study in a middy blouse by Steichen. Above, another pose from the 1927 sittings.

Portrait by Nikolai Fechin

House at Sixth and Seward, Red Cloud; home of the Charles Cathers after 1904

*With Roscoe Cather's daughters:
in front, the twins,
Margaret and Elizabeth;
in back, Virginia*

Charles Cather, Willa, Mrs. Cather, and Douglass

Isabelle and Jan Hambourg

Willa Cather with Yehudi Menuhin and his father, Pasadena, 1931

In 1930 Willa Cather met the Menuhin family through the Hambourgs in Paris. The children —Yehudi, Hephzibah, and Yaltah —were amazing as musical prodigies, but they were dear to her especially for themselves.

Doctor of Science, of Letters, of Laws, of Humanities

At Princeton University, June 1931. Left to right: Col. Charles Lindbergh,
former Secretary of State Frank B. Kellogg, President John Grier Hibben,
Willa Cather, former Secretary of War Newton D. Baker

When Willa Cather said that life had given her most of what
she had wanted, she probably was not thinking of public honors,
though she had gathered enough of them to affirm one kind of success. She received honorary degrees from the University of Nebraska (1917), the University of Michigan (1924), Creighton
(1928), Columbia (1928), Yale (1929), the University of California (1931), Princeton (1931), and Smith (1933). The first
woman to be accorded this honor by Princeton, she was cited
there as "journalist, editor and novelist," and praised for her
"inexorable sense of truth and a quality of exquisite rightness in
her limpid English prose." Other honors included the Howells
Medal for fiction from the American Academy of Arts and Letters, 1931; being named one of the "Twelve Greatest American
Women" by *Good Housekeeping,* 1931; and the Prix Femina Améri-
cain, awarded in 1933 for her achievement in *Shadows on the Rock.*

The view from Willa Cather's window: Fish weir, Bay of Fundy, Grand Manan

"Nobody can paint the sun, or sunlight. He can only paint the tricks that shadows play with it, or what it does to forms."

Grand Manan was morning, with the sun rising over the fish weir; it was a rock with its depth in an unmeasured sea. Grand Manan helped when her family began to dissolve— her father died in 1928, her mother in 1931. Age was countered by youth, weakness by strength.

On the embankment at the rear of the cottage

Timber Ridge, near Gore, Virginia

Memorial window,
Episcopal Church, Red Cloud

Willa Cather would go back as far as Virginia for her last book, crossing old bridges, opening old doors, to bring her own past more clearly into the light. Meanwhile she sketched the story of herself and her mother and grandmother in "Old Mrs. Harris," collected with other Nebraska stories ("Neighbour Rosicky" and "Two Friends") in *Obscure Destinies* (1932). The family gave stained glass windows honoring their parents to Red Cloud's Episcopal Church, which Willa Cather had joined in 1922.

570 Park Avenue, New York City, and the doorman, Gilbert Rutledge

Willa Cather and Edith Lewis moved to 570 Park Avenue in 1931; doorman Gilbert Rutledge soon learned that Miss Cather liked privacy. She was often ill, had trouble with her hand, but she wrote *Lucy Gayheart* (1935), set in Nebraska and Chicago; *Sapphira and the Slave Girl* (1940); and the stories collected in *The Old Beauty and Others* (1948). But life was diminishing: Isabelle and Douglass both died in 1938, Roscoe in 1945.

Taken December 7, 1936

Willa Cather on her sixty-third birthday

Alfred A. Knopf

Edith Lewis

New York City, May 1944: S. S. McClure, Willa Cather, Theodore Dreiser, and Paul Robeson

Willa Cather received the Gold Medal for Fiction of the National Institute of Arts and Letters on May 19, 1944. On the same occasion her old friend S. S. McClure was given the Order of Merit for services to American literature and journalism.

Three years later, on April 24, 1947, Willa Cather died at her apartment in New York City.

II. Willa Cather's America

The Midlands

"I cannot produce my kind of work
away from the American idiom.
It touches springs of memory . . . ."

Willa Cather's personal encounter with the New World of Nebraska was a microcosm of the American frontier experience—first the erasure of self by the great sky and the great silences, then a sense of the future: if the land was "not a country at all," it was "the material out of which countries are made." The lasting effect on Willa Cather, however, was a primitive sense of place. "By the end of the first autumn," she said, "that shaggy grass country had gripped me with a passion I have never been able to shake." In *O Pioneers!* and *My Ántonia* she best recreates the sense of rising glory she felt in those plains as the land responded—a world of sun and air and earth intermingled. She remembered a country of buffalo wallows grown round with yellow coreopsis, and sunflowers along the wild roads that looped across the prairie. The history of the land shone, too. "There are only two or three human stories," she wrote, "and they go on repeating themselves as fiercely as if they had never happened before." In the change from wilderness to ordered fields, Willa Cather found the most exciting story she had to tell.

Cutting wheat: Webster County

"The windy springs and the blazing summers,
one after another, had enriched and
mellowed that flat tableland; all the human
effort that had gone into it was coming
back in long, sweeping lines of fertility.
The changes seemed beautiful and
harmonious to me; it was like watching
the growth of a great man
or of a great idea."

Road going north from the Republican River to the Divide

"When the road began to climb the first long swells of the Divide, Alexandra hummed an old Swedish hymn . . . . For the first time, perhaps, since that land emerged from the waters of geologic ages, a human face was set toward it with love and yearning."

In the Cather novels the farms on the Divide and around Black Hawk or Hanover or Frankfort were settled by immigrants like Jim Burden's Virginia grandparents and the Bohemian Shimerdas and Cuzaks in *My Ántonia*; by Swedish Alexandra Bergson, with Norwegians and French Canadians, in *O Pioneers!*; and, in *One of Ours*, by Claude Wheeler's father, who came from back east. These varied pioneers marked the plains of midland America, their farms shaped by two generations of work and weather. As Virgil in the *Georgics* described the country ways of men with crops and cattle and bees, so Willa Cather wrote of these common lives—clarified, in simple lines, like the "picture writing" (says Jim Burden) of a plow seen in evening light, enlarged and contained in the circle of the sun. Her images are of a wild land that gains definition—"the gilded weather-vanes on the big red barns wink at each other across the green and brown and yellow fields." Jim Burden reads what Virgil said: "I shall be the first . . . to bring the Muse into my country."

The country of O Pioneers!

"She had never known before how much the country meant to her.
The chirping of the insects down in the long grass had been like
the sweetest music. She had felt as if her heart were hiding down there,
somewhere, with the quail and the plover and all the little wild things
that crooned or buzzed in the sun. Under the long shaggy ridges,
she felt the future stirring."

"The houses on the Divide were small and were usually tucked away in low places . . . . Most of them were built of the sod itself, and were only the unescapable ground in another form."

Dugout of the 1880's

"The red of the grass made all the great prairie the colour of wine-stains."

Red grass

Young wheat

"All over the dusty, tan-coloured wheatfields there was a tender mist of green,—millions of little fingers reaching up and waving lightly in the sun."

"One looks out over a vast checker-board, marked off in squares of wheat and corn; light and dark, dark and light."

Varicolored fields

"'There's Ivar's big pond!' Alexandra pointed to a shining sheet
of water that lay at the bottom of a shallow draw."

"The light steel windmills
tremble throughout their
frames and tug at their
moorings, as they vibrate in
the wind that often blows
from one week's end to
another across that high,
active, resolute stretch
of country."

".. . the clear blue and gold of the sky,
the evening star, the purr of the milk into
the pails, the grunts and squeals of the pigs
fighting over their supper. I began to feel the
loneliness of the farm-boy at evening,
when the chores seem everlastingly the same,
and the world so far away."

".. . a spring plowing in that country, where the furrows of a single field
often lie a mile in length, and the brown earth, with such a strong,
clean smell, and such a power of growth and fertility in it,
yields itself eagerly to the plow."

Pumpkin patch in a cornfield

"There we have short, bitter winters; windy, flower-laden springs;
long, hot summers; triumphant autumns that last until Christmas—
a season of perpetual sunlight, blazing blue skies, and frosty nights.
In this newest part of the New World autumn is the season of beauty
and sentiment, as spring is in the Old World."

"Winter has settled down over the Divide again; the season in which
Nature recuperates, in which she sinks to sleep between the
fruitfulness of autumn and the passion of spring."

Winter on the Divide

Music-box described in O Pioneers!

"'If the world were no wider than my cornfields, if there were not
  something beside this, I wouldn't feel that it was much worth while
  to work.'"

Life is not ordinary in the Nebraska novels. So many people are
from far away and the exotic comes near: we can smell the dried
mushrooms Ántonia's family brought from Bohemia. Marie
Shabata has a Turkish doll, a marvelous mechanical lady who can
smoke (the real doll described in *O Pioneers!*, shown above). And
peoples' lives contrast sharply: Alexandra in *O Pioneers!* develops
her farms, but her brother Emil and his love, Marie, are murdered
by Marie's husband. The drama of small towns is sometimes their
very familiarity, but their boundaries must continually give way
to the impulse of youth, as Thea Kronborg leaves Moonstone,
Lucy Gayheart wants to leave Haverford, and Jim Burden circles
away from Black Hawk before he returns to his own self.

The streets of Red Cloud

"In little towns, lives roll along so close to one another; loves and hates beat about, their wings almost touching. On the sidewalks along which everybody comes and goes, you must, if you walk abroad at all, at some time pass within a few inches of the man who cheated and betrayed you, or the woman you desire more than anything else in the world. Her skirt brushes against you. You say good-morning, and go on."

Recreation of a Red Cloud hotel, Stuhr Museum,
Grand Island, Nebraska

One can walk through the streets of Red Cloud and recall scenes in *The Song of the Lark, Lucy Gayheart, My Ántonia,* and other stories. The Miner house and family (the Harlings) and the "Boys' Home Hotel" are centers of life in the Black Hawk scenes of *My Ántonia.* One of Willa Cather's own scrapbooks—made of cloth with a blue cover in a circus design—is described when Jim Burden makes one for Ántonia's sister Yulka (the original scrapbook is pictured opposite, top left). Although Willa Cather's fictional characters are drawn and mixed from many sources, she often used as a central thread the story of someone she knew. Ántonia's life is based on that of Annie Sadilek Pavelka, whom Willa Cather had known and admired since Annie was the Miners' hired girl. A woman like that who cooked and sewed and took pains, and who loved a large family, was indeed an artist.

Scrapbook described in My Ántonia

Patchwork quilt

Kitchen harvest

Kolaches

"Your memories are like the colors in paints,
but you must arrange them."

"[Ántonia] had only to stand in the orchard, to put her hand on a little crab tree and look up at the apples, to make you feel the goodness of planting and tending and harvesting at last. . . . It was no wonder that her sons stood tall and straight. She was a rich mine of life, like the founders of early races."

Emil, son of Annie Pavelka ("My Ántonia")

Orchard at Inavale, west of Red Cloud

PRAIRIE SPRING

Evening and the flat land,
Rich and somber and always silent;
The miles of fresh-plowed soil,
Heavy and black, full of strength and harshness;
The growing wheat, the growing weeds,
The toiling horses, the tired men;
The long, empty roads,
Sullen fires of sunset, fading,
The eternal, unresponsive sky.
Against all this, Youth,
Flaming like the wild roses,
Singing like the larks over the plowed fields,
Flashing like a star out of the twilight;
Youth with its insupportable sweetness,
Its fierce necessity,
Its sharp desire;
Singing and singing,
Out of the lips of silence,
Out of the earthy dusk.

Beth Pavelka, granddaughter of "My Ántonia"

Lyra Garber   *Governor Silas Garber*

The charm of *A Lost Lady* is in part its central figure, Marian Forrester, wife of Captain Forrester, pioneer railroad man of Sweet Water, Nebraska, and the West. The Forrester prototypes were Silas Garber, Nebraska's fourth governor, and his wife; their hospitable house was east of Red Cloud on a hill planted with cottonwoods. Willa Cather had loved Mrs. Garber and her beguiling ways; it is her personality, if not all the details of her life, that is captured so vibrantly in Mrs. Forrester. In the novel Niel Herbert idealizes this lady, but even if spring mornings fade into the light of common day, Niel in his maturity thinks of her and her husband with affection, as ones who taught him the beauty and strength of life. To Niel the Forresters represented a more generous pioneer time; his world had fallen to ugly profiteers like Ivy Peters. This new generation is also suggested in *One of Ours* by Claude Wheeler's brothers—Bayliss, the implement dealer, and Ralph, whose cellar is filled with a clutter of broken machinery: old batteries, old bicycles, and a stereopticon with a broken lens.

The road to the Forrester place as described in A Lost Lady

"She had always the power of suggesting
things much lovelier than herself,
as the perfume of a single flower may
call up the whole sweetness of spring."

"This was the very end of the road-making West . . . . It was already
gone, that age; nothing could ever bring it back. The taste and
smell and song of it, the visions those men had seen in the air and
followed,—these [Niel] had caught in a kind of afterglow in
their own faces,—and this would always be his."

SILAS
GARBER
1833–1905

Chicago Historical Society photograph of Michigan Avenue looking north from Adams Street, 1900–1905

In the Cather novels Chicago is where aspiring musicians like Thea Kronborg or Lucy Gayheart go to study, sing in church choirs, or accompany other artists. Girls like Thea and Lucy are enchanted by the metropolitan splendors—shops of jewels and flowers, the music of the opera or of orchestras led by Theodore Thomas—but they hardly notice "the crash and scramble of that big, rich, appetent Western city." Though Chicago has its pretenders, for youth and art it is a city of possibilities. One remembers moments in *The Song of the Lark* or *Lucy Gayheart:* walks along Michigan Avenue with the lake just beyond; Clement Sebastian in the orange-red light of late afternoon, pausing by one of the bronze lions of the Art Institute (shown above); or, inside the museum, Thea engrossed with sculptures and casts and favorite paintings. In *The Professor's House,* Godfrey and Lillian St. Peter stay in Chicago at the Blackstone, their rooms overlooking the lake. When they attend the opera *Mignon,* the music recalls their youth and "the time of sweet, impersonal emotions."

Lake Michigan: "The blue floor of the Lake, wrinkled with gold"

Lake Michigan was memory and life to Godfrey St. Peter. He had been born by those blue waters (the inland sea of his childhood), had been homesick for it during the years away, and had returned to live near its shores where he could swim and sail and be healed. From the window of his attic study he could still see a blue smear of it on the horizon. It was a sign of freedom, a source of happiness.

Eva King Case

Some of Willa Cather's later stories are about family and friends, in whose obscure destinies are sudden losses, like the death of young Lesley Ferguesson after a blizzard, or deep affections. In "The Best Years" Lesley's teacher, Evangeline Knightly, is a portrait of one of Willa Cather's own teachers, Mrs. Eva King Case, who, she said, was the first person she had loved outside her family. "Neighbour Rosicky," "The Best Years," and "Old Mrs. Harris" show what she called the "accords and antipathies" of family life and the interrelationships of young and old. The houses and rooms of the last two stories depict the Cather home in Red Cloud, most vividly Grandma Boak's room and the attic where the children played and slept—"a hall, in the old baronial sense." The three generations of women in "Old Mrs. Harris"— grandmother, mother, and daughter—evoke the women of Willa Cather's family. Their lives contrast, old Mrs. Harris retreating into one room, Victoria beset by childbearing, and young Vickie brooding and wandering (and perhaps writing), in her fashion.

Grandma Boak

Willa's room seen from the side yard

Jennie Cather

Grandma's room

The way Vickie must go is determined by a chance meeting and the pull of her own blood: She is encouraged to go to college by an archeologist on a project at a nearby dig, and she is quietly helped by her grandmother, who finds the money for her future. Above is the room of old Mrs. Harris (Grandma Boak), as recreated in the Cather house. Below is "Bone Gully," a fossil bed near Red Cloud, which has yielded bones of pre-Ice Age mastodons, three-toed horses, and turtles.

"Bone Gully"

The attic

"The roof shingles were old and had curled under hot summer suns. In a driving snowstorm the frozen flakes sifted in through all those little cracks, sprinkled the beds and the children, melted on their faces, in their hair! . . . The rest of you was snug and warm under blankets and comforters, with a hot brick at one's feet. The wind howled outside; sometimes the white light from the snow and the half-strangled moon came in through the single end window."

Nebraska blizzard

Father and sons

"It was as if Rosicky had a special gift for loving people, something that was like an ear for music or an eye for colour."

"It was a nice graveyard, Rosicky reflected, sort of snug, and homelike, not cramped or mournful,—a big sweep all round it. A man could lie down in the long grass and see the complete arch of the sky over him, hear the wagons go by; in summer the mowing-machine rattled right up to the wire fence. And it was so near home."

Catherton Cemetery

The Southwest

Potsherds, Walnut Canyon, Arizona

"The stream and the broken pottery: what was any art but an effort
to make a sheath, a mould in which to imprison for a moment the
shining, elusive element which is life itself—life hurrying past
us and running away, too strong to stop, too sweet to lose?"

To Willa Cather, the Southwest meant space and color, great
rocks and mesas carved by centuries of wind and water, and, in its
canyons, cliff dwellings that recorded a once striving but lost civilization. The shells and designs of ancient pottery were in the
American idiom. With *The Song of the Lark* in 1915, her fictional
scenes move first to the sandhills and blue mountains of Colorado
and Wyoming. Near Laramie, the old wagon-ruts of the Mormon
and Forty-Niner trails stir Thea Kronborg's imagination. Later, in
the cliff dwellings of "Panther Canyon" in Arizona, her understanding of art is simplified and deepened as she feels joined to the
rituals of history. To her the ceremonies of belief, of desire, of
human necessity, are expressed in the natural symbols of eagle and
stream and sunlit rock, the elemental translated through a long
human past into art.

Point Lookout, Mesa Verde, Colorado

"And the air . . .
it was like breathing the sun,
breathing the colour of the sky."

Thea Kronborg's experience in Panther Canyon and its cliff dwellings meant a personal realization of herself as an artist. Similarly, in *The Professor's House* Tom Outland brought to midwest Hamilton and to the family of Godfrey St. Peter—along with turquoises and artifacts of the Southwest—a powerful sense of his own identity. To Tom Outland the rock cities he had discovered clustered in canyons of the Blue Mesa demonstrated man's civilizing impulse, his desire for beauty and symmetry; but, even more, they extended his definition of American history and his place in it: These objects, these rooms, even the human remains, were elements distinctively our own, something that changed a new, raw country into one with cycles of civilization throughout an ancient past. For Tom, summer on the Blue Mesa was a religious experience, an extension of his life.

Once, long before *The Professor's House*, Willa Cather had begun her high school Commencement oration in Red Cloud with this statement: "All human history is a record of an emigration, an exodus from barbarism to civilization." Since then she had observed that such emigrations are sometimes marked by cycles of success and defeat; yet, to Tom Outland, even that kind of past reinterpreted and revalued history.

Cliff Palace, Mesa Verde, Colorado

" 'Like you, I feel a reverence for this place. Wherever humanity has
made that hardest of all starts and lifted itself out of mere brutality,
is a sacred spot. Your people were cut off here without the influence of
example or emulation, with no incentive but some natural yearning
for order and security. They built themselves into this mesa and
humanized it.' "

Archbishop Lamy

The Southwest of *Death Comes for the Archbishop* (New Mexico and Arizona) is the Great Diocese of Father Latour and his companion Father Vaillant, French priests who come in the latter half of the nineteenth century to revitalize the Church long ago established in Mexican territory by Spanish conquerors. Their story is based on the lives of Archbishop Jean Lamy and Father Joseph Macheboeuf, though it is changed and refocused, even as legends blur away from the facts. Through a rough and sparkling, many-colored land, faith and works are carried by the pioneer priests—along with memories of their youth in France—to the final building in Santa Fe of Archbishop Latour's golden cathedral (the color of Avignon's Palace of the Popes). The New World has absorbed him, and become home. We journey for great distances, to Ácoma or Laguna or Isleta or Pecos, whose wall predated Coronado. On the way, the river bluffs of Willa Cather's childhood dissolve into the reality of the Mesa Encantada, and as in pioneer Nebraska, but in more striking contrasts, cultures of the Southwest intermingle (Mexican, Indian, Spanish, French). The Archbishop learns to respect other ways and other gods. Through labor and miracles his Southwest is colonized, not by cities but by time and understanding.

Ruins of eighteenth-century church at Pecos Pueblo, New Mexico

".. . long rock ridges of dead pueblo,—empty houses ruined by weather
and now scarcely more than piles of earth and stone. . . . This was all
that was left of the rich and populous Cicuyè of Coronado's expedition.
. . . It was from here, the story went, that they set forth in the spring
on their ill-fated search for the seven golden cities of Quivera."

Laguna Pueblo Church—"painted above and about the altar with gods of wind and rain and thunder, sun and moon"

" 'The Miracles of the Church seem to me to rest not so much upon faces
or voices or healing power coming suddenly near to us from afar off,
but upon our perceptions being made finer, so that for a moment our
eyes can see and our ears can hear what is there about us always.' "

Cream-colored mules

Father Latour and Father Vaillant find landscapes of red conical hills or green miracles by hidden streams, the bright air of morning or winter storms or dark caves. In their own way, too, they are light and dark. Father Vaillant displays unpriestlike guile but Christian intensity as he persuades a parishioner to give him two cream-colored mules for missionary journeys. The mules' names, he is told, " 'are Contento and Angelica, and they are as good as their names. . . . They are very companionable. They are always ridden together and have a great affection for each other.' "

"[The Bishop] was quite willing to believe that behind Jacinto there was a long tradition, a story of experience, which no language could translate to him."

"They leaped the stream like arrows speeding from the bow, and regarded the Bishop as they passed him with their mocking, humanly intelligent smile. . . . Though the goat had always been the symbol of pagan lewdness, he told himself that their fleece had warmed many a good Christian, and their rich milk nourished sickly children."

The Mesa Encantada

"Every mesa was duplicated by a cloud mesa, like a reflection, which
lay motionless above it or moved slowly up from behind it. These
cloud formations seemed to be always there, however hot and blue the
sky. Sometimes they were flat terraces, ledges of vapour; sometimes
they were dome-shaped, or fantastic, like the tops of silvery pagodas,
rising one above another, as if an oriental city lay directly behind the
rock. The great tables of granite set down in an empty plain were
inconceivable without their attendant clouds, which were a part of them,
as the smoke is part of the censer, or the foam of the wave."

Navajo hogan, Navajo Reservation, near Greasewood, Arizona

"It was the Indian manner to vanish into the landscape, not to stand out
against it. The Hopi villages that were set upon rock mesas
were made to look like the rock on which they sat, were imperceptible
at a distance. The Navajo hogans, among the sand and willows,
were made of sand and willows."

Virgin in St. Augustine Church, Isleta Pueblo, New Mexico

". . . the high colour that was in landscape and
gardens, in the flaming cactus and the gaudily
decorated altars,—in the agonized Christs and
dolorous Virgins and the very human figures of the
saints. [The Bishop] had already learned that with
this people religion was necessarily theatrical."

Santa Fe Cathedral

" 'To fulfil the dreams of one's youth;
that is the best that can happen to a man.
No worldly success can take the place of
that.' "

The Northeast and the South

Bishop Laval

"To me the rock of Quebec is not only a stronghold on
which many strange figures have for a little time cast a shadow
in the sun; it is the curious endurance of a kind of
culture, narrow but definite."

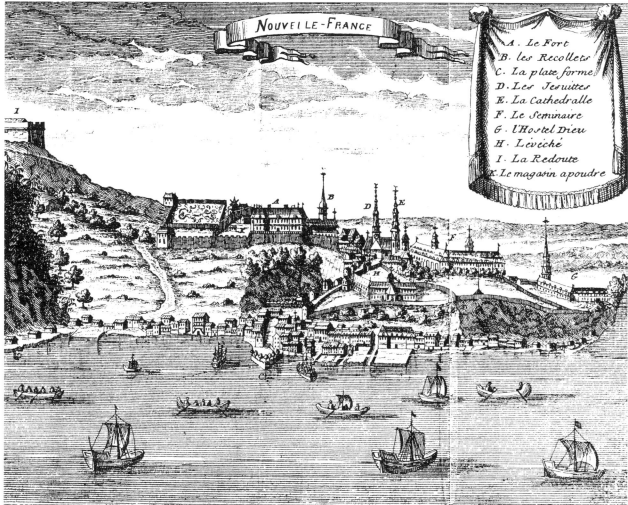

NOUVELLE-FRANCE

A . Le Fort
B . les Recollets
C . La plate forme
D . Les Jesuittes
E . La Cathedralle
F . Le Seminaire
G . l'Hostel Dieu
H . L'évéché
I . La Redoute
K . Le magasin apoudre

Engraving of Quebec at the end of the seventeenth century

Quebec in 1697 is the setting of *Shadows on the Rock*—a small,
civilized world on the edge of impenetrable forests and sometimes
impassable seas, where the traditions of the Church and French
life are held dear. But this rock is hardly serene: there are dangers
and excesses on every hand. It is another act in the story of the
American frontier, but played close to the family fire so that we
can feel how life is preserved and developed.

La Maison St. Pierre, Beaumont, Quebec

"These coppers, big and little, these brooms and clouts and brushes, were tools; and with them one made, not shoes or cabinet-work, but life itself. One made a climate within a climate; one made the days,—the complexion, the special flavour, the special happiness of each day as it passed; one made life."

Quebec Seminary, founded by Bishop Laval in 1663, Quebec City

"Whenever she heard the early bell, . . . she felt a peculiar sense of
  security, as if there must be powerful protection for Kebec in such
  steadfastness, and the new day, which was yet darkness, was beginning
  as it should. The punctual bell and the stern old Bishop who rang it
  began an orderly procession of activities and held life together on the
  rock, though the winds lashed it and the billows of snow drove over it."

The feeling of cold, rocky places of the Northeast came to Willa Cather not only from Quebec but also from her home on Grand Manan. On that small island in the Bay of Fundy one could weather storms and keep warm, as well as find the morning freshness. In one of her last stories, "Before Breakfast," she looks through the eyes of elderly Henry Grenfell, watching the sunrise (as Willa Cather herself did) from the cabin window; he is bothered by man's little distance in the great stretch of ages. After a walk through spruce woods, he sees in a young girl, swimming out through the cold sea to a rock at Ashburton Head, the epitome of the life force. "Plucky youth," he reflects, "is more bracing than enduring age."

Ashburton Head, Grand Manan, New Brunswick

Waterfall, Grand Manan

"The water was rushing down the deep-cut channel
with sound and fury till it leaped hundreds of feet
over the face of the cliff and fell into the sea: a white
waterfall that never rested."

Gulls, Grand Manan

"The sea-gulls, that seem so much creatures of the free wind and waves,
that are as homeless as the sea (able to rest upon the tides and ride the
storm, needing nothing but water and sky), at certain seasons even
they go back to something they have known before; to remote islands
and lonely ledges that are their breeding-grounds."

The millhouse and mill, Gore, Virginia

When Willa Cather returned to Virginia in *Sapphira and the Slave Girl,* she drew on memories held through a lifetime to recreate the Southern landscape of Back Creek Valley. Although by the late 1930s, when she was writing the book, she had found many disappointing changes in the South she had known as a child, a strong imagination could recombine elements to portray the earlier society of 1856—an America balanced precariously between slavery and freedom. In her story of Sapphira and Henry Colbert and their "slave girl" Nancy, the surface of life is given an easy grace that barely covers the violence and cruelty and confusion she saw in the ante-bellum South. Scenes are in the large Colbert house and mill, which still stand near Back Creek, and in the haying meadows and flowering mountain roads beyond the millhouse grounds, through the Hollow and up Timber Ridge. We catch glimpses of Willa Cather's family and friends; and in the Epilogue she places herself in the scene as a five-year-old child—eager, determined, intense—back at last in Willow Shade.

Veranda of the millhouse

"Every afternoon Mrs. Colbert was brought into the parlour and sat
here for several hours before supper. Here she could watch the light
of the sinking sun burn on the great cedars that grew along the
farther side of the creek, across from the mill. In winter weather,
when the snow was falling over the flower garden and the hedges,
that long room, with its six windows and its warm hearth,
was a pleasant place to be."

Dogwood, on the way to Timber Ridge, Virginia

"From out the naked grey wood the dogwood thrust its crooked forks
    starred with white blossoms—the flowers set in their own wild way
    along the rampant zigzag branches. Their unexpectedness,
    their singular whiteness, never loses its wonder . . . . In all the rich
    flowering and blushing and blooming of a Virginia spring,
    the scentless dogwood is the wildest thing and yet the most austere,
    the most unearthly."

Epitaph

"If [the writer] achieves anything noble, anything enduring,
it must be by giving himself absolutely to his material. . . .
He fades away into the land and people of his heart,
he dies of love only to be born again."

Willa Cather's grave, Jaffrey, New Hampshire

"The golden bough"—Nebraska cottonwood

Picture Credits

In the picture credits listed below, top and bottom are indicated by (t) and (b). Abbreviations: NSHS for Nebraska State Historical Society; NYPL for New York Public Library; WCPM for Willa Cather Pioneer Memorial and Educational Foundation; WC for Willa Cather.

Facing title page—Lucia Woods

PART I

3—Lucia Woods. 5—(t) Lucia Woods. (b) WCPM (2). 6—Lucia Woods. 7—WCPM (3). 8, 9, 10, 11—Lucia Woods. 12—(t) Bernice Slote. (b) NSHS. 13, 14—Lucia Woods. 16—WCPM. 17—Lucia Woods. 18-19—WCPM. 20—Webster County Historical Museum. 21—Roscoe and Jessica, WCPM. Douglass and James, Cather Family. 22, 23, 24—Lucia Woods. 25—Opera House, Lucia Woods. Carrie Miner and *Beauty and the Beast*, WCPM. WC and friends, NSHS. 26—(t) Cather Family. (b) Lucia Woods. 27, 28, 29—Lucia Woods. 30—WCPM. 31, 32—NSHS (4). 33—(t) Department of Special Collections, Bailey Library, University of Vermont. (b) NSHS. 34—WC (2), Cather Family. Chicago scene, Chicago Historical Society. 35—Picnic group, WCPM. Elsie and Jack, Cather Family. 36—NSHS (3). 37, 38—Carnegie Library of Pittsburgh. 39—Isabelle McClung, Cather Family. Nevin, from *Ethelbert Nevin* by John Tasker Howard, Copyright 1955 by John Tasker Howard, Copyright renewed 1963. By permission of Thomas Y. Crowell, Inc. Publisher. Boardinghouse, Bernice Slote. 40—Lucia Woods. 41—Editorial Photocolor Archives/N.Y. 42—Bernice Slote (2). 43—WCPM (2). Depot, Lucia Woods. 44—(t) Lucia Woods. (b) Souvenir brochure. New York: Harper & Bros., 1905. 45—NYPL. 46—WC, The Bettmann Archive, Inc. McClure, Lilly Library, University of Indiana. 47—Madison Square, The Clarence J. Davies Collection, Museum of the City of New York. Modjeska, NYPL. 48—Lucia Woods. 49—By permission of The Boston Athenaeum. From *Memories of a Hostess: A Chronicle of Eminent Friendships* by M. A. DeWolfe Howe. Boston: Little, Brown & Co., 1922. 51—Bernice Slote (2). 52—Edith Lewis's print of Aimé Dupont photo, courtesy of Mrs. Emmeline Ruddy. 53—Cather Family. 54—David E. Scherman. 55—Lucia Woods. 56—Elizabeth Sergeant, Katharine S. White. Isabelle McClung, Cather Family. Fremstad, NYPL. 57, 58—Cather Family. 59—(t) Cather Family. (b) Bernice Slote. 60—(t) WCPM. (b) U.S. War Department General Staff Photo, National Archives. 61—Scherril Schell photo from unidentified clipping, Cather Family. 62, 63—Cather Family (4). 64—(t) Cather Family. (b) Photographers Associated, courtesy of Omaha Public Library. 65—Mrs. Fisher, Department of Special Collections, Bailey Library, University of Vermont. Zoë Akins, reproduced by permission of The Huntington Library, San Marino, California. WC and friends, Lilly Library, University of Indiana. 66—(t) Cather Family. (b) Lucia Woods. 67—Cather Family (4). 68—(t) Steichen photo, Cather Family. (b) Nikolai Fechin portrait bequeathed by WC to Helen Cather Southwick, Peter A. Juley & Son photo from WCPM. 69—Cather house, WCPM. WC and nieces, Brown Brothers. WC with parents and Douglass, WCPM. 70—The Hambourgs, Cather Family. WC and Menuhins, Graham photo from *California Life* clipping, Cather Family. WC in mortarboard, Keystone. 71—Princeton University Archives. 72—(t) Philip L. Southwick. (b) Cather Family. 73, 74—Lucia Woods (3). 75—H. Foster Ensminger photo of WC, Cather Family. Passport photo of Edith Lewis, courtesy of Mrs. Emmeline Ruddy. Knopf photo by Harold Strauss. 76—Wide World Photo.

PART II

All pictures in Part II are by Lucia Woods except the following: 84—(t) NSHS. (b) C. Bertrand and Marian Schultz. 89—David E. Scherman. © 1951 by Time Inc. 96—Lyra Garber, WCPM. Silas Garber, NSHS. 100—Chicago Historical Society. 102—WCPM. 103—Mrs. Boak, Cather Family. Mrs. Cather, WCPM. 105—(b) David E. Scherman. 106—(b) David E. Scherman. © 1951 by Time Inc. 119—Engraving, no credit. 122, 123—Philip L. Southwick (3).
N.B. The locale of the photograph on page 97, representing the road to the Forrester house in *A Lost Lady*, is Gore, Virginia, not Red Cloud, Nebraska.

For courtesies shown her while she was making photographs for this book, Lucia Woods thanks the following: In Virginia—Mr. and Mrs. Charles Poole, owners of Willow Shade; the Lucas Family, owners of the Millhouse; Rev. Morris Cather. In Pittsburgh—Mr. and Mrs. Robert Mertz, owners of the McClung house. In New York City—Roberta Wiener; Marta Vivas. In Chicago—Frank H. Woods. In New Mexico—Mr. and Mrs. Walter Mayer (Mrs. Mayer's mother was Mrs. George H. Van Stone in whose house and garden, shown on p. 66, Willa Cather was often a guest); Gilbert Platero; Mrs. James R. Thorpe, Sr. In Nebraska—Alicia Blue; the late Mary Etta Blue; Mrs. Richard Borton; Mrs. Jerald Byrne; the Cormans of Superior; the Lyle Hendersons; Mr. and Mrs. Hugh McPartland; Emil and Beth Pavelka; Betty and Russ Peirce; Mrs. Charles Reiher; the Marvin Thayers. In Quebec City—M. Angelo Tremblay, Quebec Department of Tourism; Le Seminaire de Quebec.

Citations are keyed to the following bibliographical checklist. Date of first publication appears at the left except in the case of posthumous collections. If the edition cited is other than the first, it is indicated in the entry. Bibliographical data on interviews, uncollected work, and secondary sources are given in the citations.

UNIVERSITY OF NEBRASKA PRESS

The Kingdom of Art: Willa Cather's First Principles and Critical Statements, 1893–1896. Selected and edited with two essays and a commentary by Bernice Slote. 1966. Cited as *KA*.

The World and the Parish: Willa Cather's Articles and Reviews, 1893–1902. Selected and edited with a commentary by William M. Curtin. 2 vols. 1970.

1903   *April Twilights (1903).* Edited with an introduction by Bernice Slote. Revised edition 1968. Cited as *AT*.

Willa Cather's Collected Short Fiction, 1892–1912. Edited by Virginia Faulkner. Introduction by Mildred R. Bennett. (Includes *The Troll Garden*, first published in 1905 by McClure, Phillips & Co.). Revised edition 1970. Cited as *CSF*.

Uncle Valentine and Other Stories: Willa Cather's Uncollected Short Fiction, 1915–1929. Edited with an introduction by Bernice Slote. 1973. Cited as *UV*.

HOUGHTON MIFFLIN COMPANY

1912   *Alexander's Bridge.* [Out of print.] Cited as *AB*.

1913   *O Pioneers!* Sentry Edition, 1962. Cited as *OP*.

1915   *The Song of the Lark.* Sentry Edition, 1963. Cited as *SOL*.

1918   *My Ántonia.* Sentry Edition, 1961. Cited as *MA*.

ALFRED A. KNOPF, INC.

1920   *Youth and the Bright Medusa.* Cited as *YBM*.

1922   *One of Ours.* Cited as *OURS*.

1923   *April Twilights and Other Poems.* Cited as *ATOP*.

1923   *A Lost Lady.* Cited as *ALL*.

1925   *The Professor's House.* Cited as *TPH*.

1926   *My Mortal Enemy.* Cited as *MME*.

1927   *Death Comes for the Archbishop.* Cited as *DCA*.

1931   *Shadows on the Rock.* Cited as *SOR*.

1932   *Obscure Destinies.* Cited as *OD*.

1935   *Lucy Gayheart.* Cited as *LG*.

1936   *Not Under Forty.* Cited as *NUF*.

1940   *Sapphira and the Slave Girl.* Cited as *SSG*.

The Old Beauty and Others. 1948. Cited as *TOB*.

Willa Cather on Writing. 1949. Cited as *OW*.

PART I

8—Interview in the *Philadelphia Record*, datelined New York, August 9 [1913]. Reprinted in *KA*, p. 448. 10—*SOL*, pp. 276–77. 11—*MA*, p. 29. 13—"Nebraska: The End of the First Cycle," *Nation*, September 5, 1923, p. 237. 14—*MA*, p. ix. 17—*SOL*, p. 7. 27—*SOL*, p. 71. 28—*AT*, p. 3. 29—Commencement oration, *Red Cloud Chief*, June 13, 1890. *MA*, p. 322. 30—*MA*, p. 263. 33—"The Passing Show," *Nebraska State Journal*, March 1, 1896. Reprinted in *KA*, p. 417. 41—*OURS*, p. 343. 42—Elizabeth Shepley Sergeant, *Willa Cather: A Memoir* (Bison Book ed.; Lincoln: University of Nebraska Press, 1963), p. 96. 43—*ATOP*, p. 66. 47—*MME*, pp. 33–34, 58. 48—"The Treasure of Far Island," *New England Magazine*, October 1902. Reprinted in *CSF*, pp. 265–66. 49—*NUF*, p. 57. 51—*AB*, 43, 42. 52—Peter Lyon, *Success Story: The Life and Times of S. S. McClure* (New York: Charles Scribner's Sons, 1963), p. 390. *Letters of Sarah Orne Jewett*, ed. Annie Fields (Boston: Houghton Mifflin Co., 1911), pp. 248–49. 53—Mildred R. Bennett, *The World of Willa Cather* (Bison Book ed.; Lincoln: University of Nebraska Press, 1961), pp. 200–201. *SOL*, p. 251. 54—Sergeant, *Willa Cather*, p. 49. 60—*OURS*, p. 274. 61—"On the Art of Fiction," *OW*, p. 102. 66—Interview by Rose C. Feld, *New York Times Book Review*, December 21, 1924, p. 13. 67—Interview by Eleanor Hinman, *Lincoln Sunday Star*, November 6, 1921. 72—"Light on Adobe Walls," *OW*, pp. 123–24.

PART II

79—Interview by Walter Tuttle, *Century*, July 1925, p. 312. *MA*, p. 7. Interview, *Omaha Bee*, October 29, 1921. *OP*, 119. 81—*MA*, p. 306. 82—*OP*, p. 65. *MA*, p. 245. *OP*, p. 75. *MA*, p. 264. 83—*OP*, p. 71. 84—*OP*, p. 19. *MA*, p. 15. 85—*OURS*, p. 120. *OP*, p. 75. 86—*OP*, pp. 36, 75–76. 87—*MA*, p. 347. *OP*, p. 76. 88—"Nebraska: The End of the First Cycle," p. 236. 89—*OP*, p. 187. 90—*OP*, p. 124. 91—*LG*, p. 167. 93—Interview by Flora Merrill, *New York World*, April 19, 1925, Sec. 3, 1:2. 94—*MA*, p. 353. 95—*ATOP*, p. 56. 98—*ALL*, p. 172. 99—*ALL*, pp. 168–69. 100—*SOL*, p. 244. *TPH*, p. 93. 101—*LG*, p. 47. 102—"Katherine Mansfield," *OW*, p. 110. "The Best Years," *TOB*, p. 111. 105—"The Best Years," pp. 108–109. 106—"Neighbour Rosicky," *OD*, pp. 66, 18. 107—*SOL*, p. 378. 108—*TPH*, p. 240. Commencement oration, *Red Cloud Chief*, June 13, 1890. 109—*TPH*, p. 221. 111—*DCA*, pp. 123–24. 112—*DCA*, pp. 90, 50. 113—*DCA*, p. 60. 114—*DCA*, pp. 92, 30–31. 115—*DCA*, p. 95. 116—*DCA*, p. 233. 117—*DCA*, p. 142. 118—*DCA*, p. 261. 119—"On *Shadows on the Rock*," *OW*, p. 15. 120—*SOR*, p. 198. 121—*SOR*, p. 105. 122—"Before Breakfast," *TOB*, p. 166. 123—"Before Breakfast," p. 162. "Two Friends," *OD*, pp. 193–94. 125—*SSG*, p. 41. 126—*SSG*, pp. 115–16. 127—"The Best Stories of Sarah Orne Jewett," *OW*, p. 51.

Acknowledgments

The University of Nebraska Press wishes to express its gratitude to the family of Willa Cather for its kindness in allowing us to use many of the pictures in this book. Our particular thanks go to Mrs. Philip L. Southwick (Helen Cather), who has worked with us on this project since its inception; to Charles E. Cather, Trustee of the Estate of Willa Cather, for permission to reproduce a portion of the manuscript of "Dogs" and to quote from "Nebraska: The End of the First Cycle" by Willa Cather; and to Mrs. Richard S. Shannon, Jr. (Margaret Cather) for assistance with picture identification. We are grateful to Mrs. Mildred R. Bennett, President, Willa Cather Pioneer Memorial and Educational Foundation, who also has helped us from the beginning and has made available the picture archives of the WCPM; and to William A. Koshland, Chairman of the Board, Alfred A. Knopf, Inc., for his friendly and invaluable aid and counsel on this and other Willa Cather projects.

Special thanks go to Professor Philip L. Southwick, Carnegie-Mellon University, and to the following members of the Board of Governors of the Willa Cather Pioneer Memorial for permission to include their photographs in this book: David E. Scherman, Editor, Time Incorporated Book Clubs; Professor C. Bertrand Schultz, University of Nebraska–Lincoln, and Mrs. Schultz; and Professor Bernice Slote, University of Nebraska–Lincoln. Others to whom we are especially indebted for assistance in collecting illustrative materials are: John Buechler, Head, Special Collections, Guy W. Bailey Library, University of Vermont; Earle E. Coleman, University Archivist, Princeton University; Julia M. Cunningham, Librarian, Pennsylvania Division, Carnegie Library of Pittsburgh; Frank Gibson, Director, Omaha Public Libraries;

Ethel Jacobsen, Picture Room, Nebraska State Historical Society; Jack Jackson, Art Department, Library of The Boston Athenaeum; Mrs. Harry Obitz, Red Cloud, Nebraska; Mrs. Paul M. Rhymer, Curator of Prints, Chicago Historical Society; Mrs. Emmeline Ruddy, New York City; and Katharine S. White (Mrs. E. B. White), North Brooklin, Maine.

During the preparation of this book many photographs were obtained which, because of space limitations, could not be included; however, all those collected by the UNP will be preserved in the archives of the Willa Cather Pioneer Memorial. For helping us to locate or providing these pictures and for collateral information we are grateful to Professor Bruce P. Baker II, University of Nebraska at Omaha; Professor James Blackman, University of Nebraska–Lincoln; Alice H. Bonnell, Curator, Columbiana, Low Library, Columbia University; Professor Neal Copple, University of Nebraska–Lincoln; Francis Cunningham, Lincoln, Nebraska; Robert Fell, Publications Editor, Creighton University; Grace B. Howes, Assistant Archivist, Smith College; J. R. K. Kantor, University Archivist, University of California, Berkeley; Evelyn M. Kent, J. B. Lippincott Company; Mary Jo Pugh, Assistant Curator, Michigan Historical Collections, University of Michigan; and Judith A. Schiff, Chief Research Archivist, Yale University Library.

We are deeply grateful to Willa Cather's publishers Houghton Mifflin Company and Alfred A. Knopf, Inc., and to Hamish Hamilton, London, for permission to include quotations from her books.

Bernice Slote wishes to acknowledge the work of Virginia Faulkner, Editor of the University of Nebraska Press, who was the editor of this book.

The table of contents offers a general chronological outline of Willa Cather's life and indicates actual and fictional locales. This index is limited to the names of individuals and titles of works discussed or quoted.

Index